Tiny Talk

Workbook

Susan Rivers

Oxford University Press

Oxford University Press
198 Madison Avenue, New York, NY 10016, USA
Great Clarendon Street, Oxford OX2 6DP, England

Oxford   New York
Athens   Auckland   Bangkok   Bogotá   Buenos Aires   Cape Town   Chennai
Dar es Salaam   Delhi   Florence   Hong Kong   Istanbul   Karachi   Kolkata
Kuala Lumpur   Madrid   Melbourne   Mexico City   Mumbai   Nairobi   Paris
São Paulo   Shanghai   Singapore   Taipei   Tokyo   Toronto   Warsaw

and associated companies in
Berlin   Ibadan

OXFORD is a trademark of Oxford University Press.

ISBN 0-19-435151-3

Editorial Manager: Shelagh Speers
Editor: Edward Yoshioka
Production Editor: Mark Steven Long
Designers: Doris Chen, Doreen Cheung
Art Buyer: Nina Hess
Production Manager: Abram Hall

Printing (last digit): 10 9 8 7

Printed in Hong Kong.

***Illustrations by* Kathleen McCord/Bookmakers, Ltd.**

Computer graphics by Eliot Bergman
Cover design by Doris Chen
Cover illustration by Kathleen McCord/Bookmakers, Ltd.

Table Of Contents

UNIT
1

A Color.

5

B Circle Benny.

C Circle Sue.

A Color.

9

B Which are the same? Circle.

C Match.

UNIT
3

A Color.

13

B Circle the girls.

C Circle the boys.

UNIT 4

A Color.

B Match.

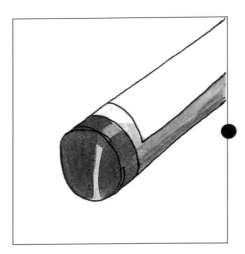 

 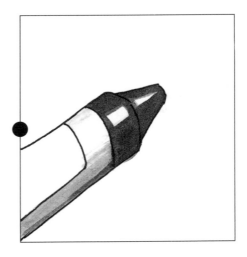

18

C Which is different? Write an X.

UNIT
5

A Color.

B Which are the same? Circle.

REVIEW UNIT 1

A Trace and color.

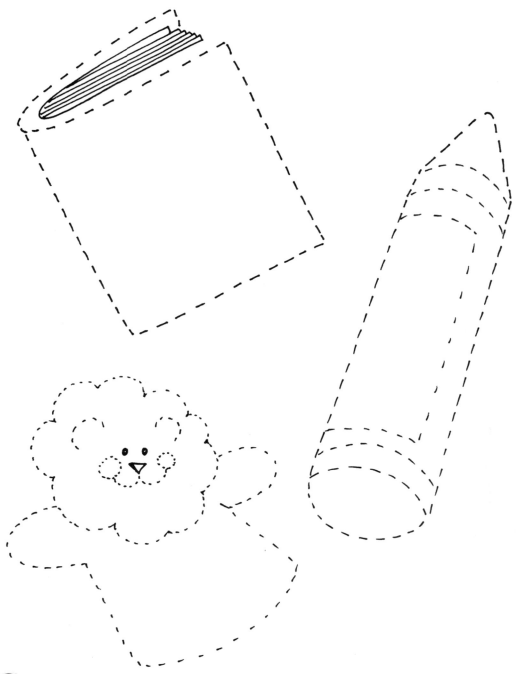

B Match.

A Color.

B Color.

C Trace and match.

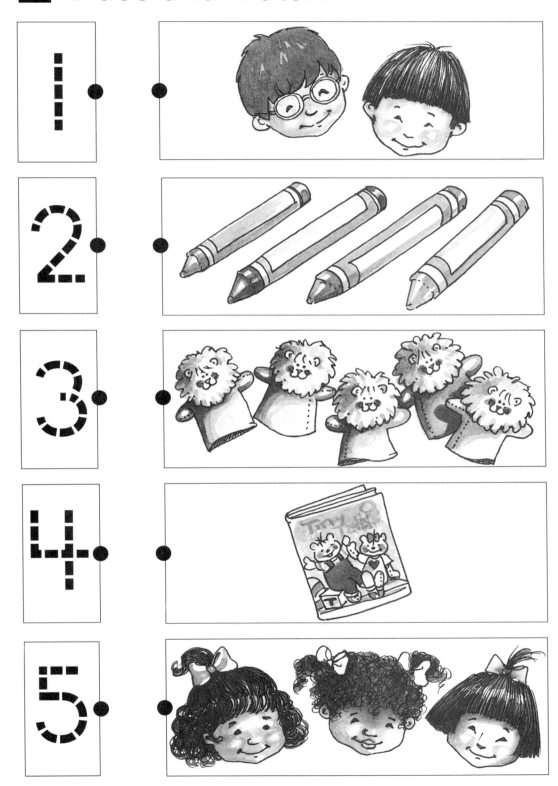

UNIT 7

A Color.

B Find the snacks.

C Which are the same? Circle.

A Color.

B Color.

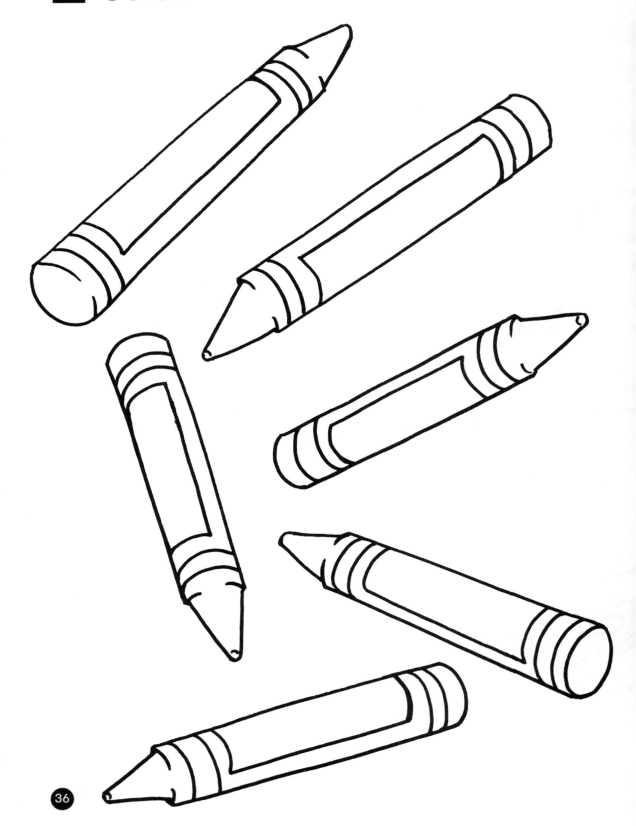

C Color.

A Color.

B Which are the same? Circle.

C Match.

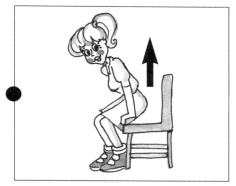

A Color.

B Match.

C Which is different? Write an X.

A Find and circle.

B Match.

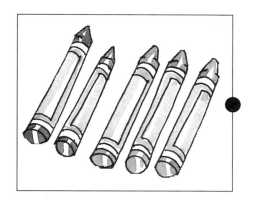

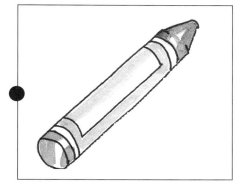

C Color.